ANCIENT FORESTS

DAVID MIDDLETON

ANCIENT FORESTS

A CELEBRATION OF
NORTH AMERICA'S
OLD-GROWTH WILDERNESS

CHRONICLE BOOKS ❦ SAN FRANCISCO

Printed in Hong Kong

Library of Congress Cataloging-in-Publication Data

Middleton, David.
    The ancient forests / by David Middleton.
        p. cm.
    ISBN 0-87701-814-6
    1. Old growth forests–Northwest, Pacific–Pictorial works.
    2. Forest ecology–Northwest, Pacific–Pictorial works. I. Title.
    QH104.5.N6M64   1992
    508.315'–dc20   91-24493
                                                             CIP

Book and cover design by Karen Pike.
Composition by T:H Typecast, Inc.

Distributed in Canada by Raincoast Books,
112 East Third Avenue, Vancouver, B.C. V5T 1C8

10 9 8 7 6 5 4 3 2 1

Chronicle Books
275 Fifth Street
San Francisco, California 94103

TO EMMA McGEE
AND MY RING COMPANIONS

ACKNOWLEDGMENTS

No large project is ever the sole effort of a single person, and a book is no exception. Many people have helped me either directly by answering my questions, providing photographs, or making suggestions or indirectly with a stimulating thought, a compelling rhythm, or simple encouragement. All of them added material to the steaming mental compost that nourished my written and pictorial garden and enabled it to flourish.

Forest scientists Paul Alaback, Jim Boyle, Rick Brown, Ed Jensen, Dave McCorkle, Gary Miller, Jerry Mires, Andy Moldenke, David Pearson, and Bob Pyle repeatedly took the time to explain the intricacies of the forest to me and untangle my thoughts.

Many other people contributed to this project. These include Mandy Coles, Marlene Finley, Jim Fitzgerald, Jeff Garver, George Lepp, Pat Loveland, Wayne Lynch, John McCutcheon, Jon Martin, Chris Maser, Gary Mozel, Eliot Norse, Dennis Paulson, Don Poole, Roy Randell, Tim Schowalter, John Shaw, Paul Simon, Tom Spies, and Doc Storm. I thank them all.

I would also like to thank my copyeditor, Mary Anne Stewart, and all the folks at Chronicle Books, especially my editor, Annie Barrows, whose patience, support, and confidence were evergreen.

CONTENTS

There is an honesty in music
that stirs you to act.
There is a rhythm
that picks up your feet and moves your mind.
There is a melody
that crosses the generations and makes you remember.
And there are harmonies that make you become.

There is music in the forest as well.
Rhythms too soft to hear,
but they stir you nonetheless.
Melodies that carry you along and
harmonies that fall on you
as you pass beneath.

This book is for all those who
live, work, play, or dream about the forest.
They know the melodies and hear the rhythms,
and the music stirs them.

PATRIARCHS OF TIME

P atriarch," "Millennium," "Sentinel," "Cathedral"—these are the names given to groves within the realm of the ancient forest. They speak of unimaginable size—the Cathedral Forest—and unfathomable age—the Millennium Grove; of primeval emotions—Shadow of the Sentinels—and spiritual reverence—Grove of the Patriarchs. Words of veneration describe this land of *ahs*.

The ancient forest stretches two thousand miles along the Pacific coast from the redwoods of Big Sur, California, to the Sitka spruce of Afognak Island in the Gulf of Alaska. Nestled between the ocean dunes and the alpine tundra of the western mountain rim, old-growth forests have been called the most magnificent coniferous forests in the world. The largest and some of the oldest trees in the world are found within these ancient groves.

While not having as many plant species as the tropical rainforest, the old-growth forest supports two to ten times more plant life—400 tons per acre in a typical old-growth forest and a remarkable 1,800 tons per acre in an old-growth redwood forest as opposed to 180 tons per acre in the tropical rainforest. If invertebrate animals of the soil are included in the diversity tally, the old-growth forests of Oregon support more animal species than any other place in the world: a section of forest floor one meter by one meter is home to two hundred thousand mites of seventy-five different species.

Old-growth forest is the primary habitat of over a hundred species of vertebrates and fifteen hundred (perhaps twice that) species of invertebrates. It is the home of the Pacific yew, an unassuming tree of the understory from which a potent anticancer drug is derived; the aplodontia, or mountain beaver, the most primitive living rodent in the world; and the Pacific giant salamander, the largest land salamander in the world. It is home to the best- and least-known bird in North America—the northern spotted owl and the marbled murrelet—both of which are threatened species dependent on old-growth forests for survival. It is also home to a daddy-longlegs that cracks open snail shells with pincers bigger than its body and to the unique-headed bug, a living fossil that is the ancestor of all true bugs. Only four specimens of this bizarre bug have been found—two in the old-growth forests of Oregon, one in Colorado, and one in Siberia. Dozens of other insect species that have never been described, let alone studied, also dwell in the high or dark or out-of-the-way corners of the old-growth forest.

Eight to ten old-growth forest communities interweave within the ancient forest realm, forming what may be thought of as three great forest kingdoms. Each kingdom has at once a subset of unique plants and animals that characterize it and a shared set of plants and animals that might be found in any old-growth forest. Western hemlock, white trillium, bald eagles, great horned owls, and varied thrushes are widely found

Above Mushroom and moss detail on the forest floor, an often overlooked sight in the forest of *ahs*.

Sitka spruce grows abundantly along the entire Northwest coast and is often associated with a sea of swordferns. Hoh Rainforest, Olympic National Park, Washington.

A Sitka spruce rising against the weathered bole of an ancient cedar snag illustrates the natural successional process from wet cedar forest to drier spruce forest. Quinalt loop trail, Olympic National Forest, Washington.

The verdant banks of Three Creek swollen with meltwater. Note the diversity of tree sizes in this Oregon old-growth forest. The large trees are mostly Douglas-fir; the smaller ones are Pacific silver fir and western hemlock.

Moss-covered limbs in Sitka
spruce forest on Afognak Island,
Alaska. Here the ancient forest
realm reaches its northern
terminus.

Western redcedar and a fallen log in the Millennium Grove, Santiam Ranger District, Oregon. Several of the trees in this cathedral forest are almost 1,000 years old, a rare age for a forest so frequently disturbed by fire, wind, and logging.

throughout the region. Ponderosa pine, tanoak, Del Norte salamanders, and brown bears are restricted to just a few localities.

The southernmost and smallest old-growth forest kingdom — the redwood forest — stretches for three hundred miles along the coast of northern California and southern Oregon, a range coinciding with the coastal summer fog belt that washes inland several miles to bathe the trees with moisture. The redwood forest is a shadowy cathedral, moist and still with luxuriant growths of mosses and ferns, little influenced by fire and wind. During summer, when rainfall is slight, fog condensation, the equivalent of sixteen inches of rain, maintains the damp environment redwoods require. Where mountains and hills restrict the reach of fog, the summer forest is too dry to support redwoods. Unfortunately, this damp home is also destroyed by logging. Single redwood giants left uncut and isolated in a field of stumps will die after a decade or so in their new, harsh, sunlit world.

Redwoods are some of the tallest trees in the world, the champion measuring 368 feet high — the length of a football field, both end zones, and a couple of rows of seats. Redwoods are long-lived as well, with some estimated to be over two thousand years old. Amazingly, for a tree whose fossil record extends far back into the millennia, very few insect pests have evolved adaptations to attack it. Often just old age, bringing with it the failure of the tree's inner transport systems, is the cause of death. High concentrations of tannic acid in the bark and needles repel most insects and discourage fungus, the principle agent of rot, making redwood highly in demand by the timber industry as an outdoor building wood. Today, less than 2 percent of the original 2 million acres of redwood forest are protected from future logging.

To the north of the redwood kingdom is the great kingdom of the Douglas-fir. This diverse forest covers the Klamath and Siskiyou mountains of northern California and southern Oregon, much of the Coast Ranges of Oregon and Washington, and the western side of the Cascade Mountains into southern

Rain droplets on a bough of Douglas-fir. Douglas-fir is the dominant tree of old-growth forests in Oregon and Washington.

Early summer cones of western hemlock, a familiar tree in old-growth forests from coastal Alaska to northern California.

Winter wraps the emerald forest in a shroud of icy stillness. Along Hackleman Creek, Oregon Cascades.

Washington. Two hundred years ago the Douglas-fir forest also grew in the fertile lowland valleys of Oregon and Washington, rivaling the redwoods in girth and height. Two centuries of civilization have all but eliminated the lowland old-growth forest, and now the remnant giants, growing on poorer, mountain soils, are considerably smaller. A typical giant Douglas-fir is four to six feet across, 250 feet high, and five hundred years old.

This kingdom is the only one that withstands a long summer drought and its companion disturbance, wildfire. Periodically through the decades a catastrophic fire will burn through an old-growth grove. Douglas-fir, though, is dependent on this type of disturbance for regeneration. Without fire, the shadowy forest floor is too dimly lit and thickly carpeted for Douglas-fir seedlings to grow, though some might get a start on the raw soil exposed by the root wads of forest giants toppled by the wind. The native mosaic of forest communities in the Douglas-fir forests was created and maintained by fire.

Other large trees less commonly found in the Douglas-fir kingdom are sugar, western white, and ponderosa pine; western redcedar; incense-cedar; and Port-Orford-cedar. The understory trees are typically western hemlock, vine maple, grand fir, and tanoak. Douglas-fir largely supports the timber industry in the Northwest, but Port-Orford-cedar is by far the most valued wood. Roughly only 10 percent of Oregon and Washington's original west-side old-growth forest remains.

The northernmost kingdom is the Sitka spruce/western hemlock forest, extending from the northern coast of Oregon through the Olympic Peninsula and the North Cascades of Washington to the coastal forests of British Columbia and southeast Alaska. Prodigious, frequent rain and moderate temperatures endow this kingdom with the world's best tree-growing climate. The world's largest Sitka spruce, Douglas-fir, western hemlock, western redcedar, subalpine fir, and Alaska-cedar grow here. A five-hundred-year-old Sitka spruce can reach four to five feet across and two hundred feet high.

The spruce/hemlock forest is part of the global temperate

Cloudscape in Olympic National Park, Washington. Clouds are an important source of water to many plants in the ancient forest. In the Oregon Cascades, cloud-drip accounts for 16 inches of precipitation annually.

Marymere Falls in summer, Olympic National Park, Washington. A short trail leads through an impressive old-growth grove to this picturesque scene.

Quartzville Creek and vine maple
boughs, central Oregon Cascades.

November vine maples in an Oregon old-growth forest. Shaded vine maples turn golden in autumn, but those in the sun are red.

Maidenhair fern is a common fern in southeastern Alaska, where it grows in thick banks of intertwining spirals.

Bunchberry, a diminutive member of the dogwood family, crowds the sun gaps of the forest floor, vying for light and attention.

Port-Orford-cedar is the rarest of the four "cedars" found in the Northwest, but it produces the most prized wood. A fatal root fungus and logging pressure combine to make this tree increasingly rare.

Early October in an Oregon old-growth forest. A Douglas-fir wrapped in the golden hues of vine maple.

rainforest biome that also includes the southern coast of Chile and parts of coastal New Zealand, Tasmania, and Japan. A temperate rainforest has cool, wet summers, no prolonged period of drought, and is not significantly influenced by fire. Wind is the primary agent of disturbance that maintains the forest diversity, knocking over small groups and single trees and building a forest mosaic on a finer scale than in the fire-maintained Douglas-fir forest.

Growing in river bottoms, Sitka spruce is the dominant tree, with western hemlock replacing it on older or drier sites. Alaska-cedar, mountain hemlock, and Douglas-fir play lesser roles in wetter and higher forests. Fewer plant species are found here than in the forests to the south, for the prolonged cool, damp growing conditions of the spruce/hemlock kingdom require specialized species. Douglas-fir and vine maple do not get much past the Canadian border, and western hemlock is found growing from treeline to the beachfront in ecological niches it would be outcompeted for farther south. The only trees on Afognak Island, the northernmost tip of the old-growth forest region, are Sitka spruce. There the old-growth forest is heavily draped in mosses, and the forest giants are thirty inches in diameter, 150 feet tall, and three hundred years old. But despite the lack of tree diversity, wildlife reigns in this forest kingdom, with world-renowned populations of brown bears, salmon, and deer.

The amount of remaining old-growth forest in the spruce/hemlock kingdom is unknown. Unfortunately, detailed mapping of the ancient forest has never been done. The typical tree-size and age-based definitions of old growth are not applicable for the relatively smaller, younger trees of the temperate rainforest old-growth. But the largest, grandest forests are known and sustain heavy logging pressure, for Sitka spruce is a strong but lightweight wood popular in the construction industry because it, along with hemlock, makes a beautiful, finished wood product.

Originally, seventy thousand square miles of old-growth forest rose between the western mountain rim and the Pacific Ocean. Sixty percent has been cut in Canada, 90 percent in the United States. The remaining unprotected significant tracts of ancient forest are endangered and disappearing as roads and clearcuts invade their boundaries. Estimates of when the last unprotected groves will be cut vary from one to four human generations. One human lifetime left for a forest that spans twenty and for a spirit that spans a hundred.

THE ANCIENT FOREST
CHAPTER ONE

What is an old-growth forest? Is it just a stand of old trees? How old? Is it a stand of large trees? How large? What does "old growth" mean? Is that big old tree out back old growth? What about those big trees down in the park? They aren't very old, but they sure are big. Are they an old-growth forest?

These are simple, direct questions that have been asked but not well answered for twenty years. Unfortunately, no simple, direct answers exist. Old-growth forests are not uniform or one-dimensional. The forests included within the ancient forest realm vary so dramatically in tree species, rainfall, snowfall, temperature, altitude, soil, and drought that one person's image of an old-growth forest probably does not coincide with another's. In general, an old-growth forest is a structurally complex forest, hundreds of years old, that has not been directly altered by humans. A young forest is a few decades old, a mature forest one hundred years old or so, but both of these forests typically lack the structural complexity characteristic of old-growth forests.

Two other words are often used to describe the old-growth forest—"virgin" and "climax." A virgin forest is not necessarily an old-growth forest. It is simply any forest that has not been directly altered by humans. Virgin forests may be naturally growing young or mature forests, as well as old-growth forests. A forest regenerating after a fire, landslide, or windstorm is a virgin forest but may not reach the old-growth stage for centuries. A climax forest is one that has reached the culminating stage of plant succession—one in which the species composition of the dominant trees will not change if left undisturbed. A species that can regenerate and replace itself in the climax forest is a climax species. Most young trees cannot compete in the environment of their parent tree because the parent tree has modified the habitat to the extent that it now favors other species over the original species.

Western hemlock, Sitka spruce, and redwood are the primary climax species in the Pacific Northwest, but aside from the California redwood groves, climax forests are rare because the major disturbance factor of fire favors the dominance of Douglas-fir. Douglas-fir is a sun-loving subclimax species that comes back in dense stands after a forest fire yet cannot regenerate in the shade of its parent trees. It therefore never reaches a climax state itself. As the Douglas-fir forest matures, the shade-tolerant western hemlock and Sitka spruce are able to take hold and thrive as young trees, but to mature past this stage into a climax forest, they need the amount of sun and space characteristic of Douglas-fir forests in which old trees have lost many of their lower branches and have begun to die and fall. Since Douglas-fir is extremely long-lived, it takes centuries for this kind of environment to develop. During this time, perhaps one-half the potential lifetime of a Douglas-fir, a major forest fire is very likely. Fire resets the forest clock and begins anew the centuries-long climb toward a climax forest. Most of the old-growth forests in the Northwest are not climax forests.

Above The red squirrel and its close relatives, the northern flying squirrel and chickaree, are abundant in the ancient forest and are important prey items for owls, hawks, martens, and bobcats.

A climax western hemlock forest in southeastern Alaska. The hemlocks are growing on rotting Sitka spruce stumps, the trees they replaced in the natural forest successional process.

The four structural components characteristic of old-growth forests—large live trees, multi-layered canopy, dead trees (snags), and downed logs. Each element plays a vital and integrated role in the ecology of ancient forest communities. Douglas-fir and western hemlock, Oregon Cascades.

The most revered aspect of the ancient forest is its large, living trees. The ancient forest realm is blessed by the best tree-growing climate in the world. Prodigious rains and moderate temperatures allow long-lived species to reach more than 250 feet in height and 6 to 8 feet or more in diameter. House Creek, Oregon Cascades.

The earliest descriptions of old-growth forests detailed the size and age of the trees—no wonder, since the sheer massiveness of these forests is initially so overwhelming. But to define an old-growth forest by the age and size of its trees alone belies the different histories and growing conditions unique to each forest. A forest high on the slopes of Mt. Hood may have trees three hundred years old that are only twenty inches in diameter and 60 feet tall. Eighty miles to the west in the Coast Range a tree twenty inches wide may be only forty-five years old but it will be over 140 feet tall. A three-hundred-year-old tree in the Coast Range might be seven feet wide and over 250 feet tall. Each of these trees may or may not be part of an old-growth forest.

Old-growth forest also tends to be defined in terms of viewpoint. Every person, agency, or constituency concerned with old-growth forest defines "old growth" to best suit its own needs—an economist by the premium price of its timber, a mill owner by the size of the blade needed to cut it, a luthier by the sound its wood produces, a cabinetmaker by the fineness of its wood grain, a forester by the diameter of its tree trunks at breast height, a zoologist by the animals it harbors, a politician by the clamor any mention of it produces. All legitimate but different definitions describing the same forest.

Given all these different perspectives, a common definition of old-growth forest is essential. To understand and appreciate the unique character of the old-growth forest we must start from common ground. Without a common definition, discussions and decisions are fruitless. Gather five people in a room and ask them a question about old growth and you will get five different answers. Each person will have a different forest in mind—each person will be using a different definition. At a time when loggers, foresters, biologists, politicians, and preservationists are grappling with hard decisions on the future of the ancient forest, a common definition of old growth becomes critical.

In the early 1980s the first comprehensive research on the ecology of the old-growth forests was published. Comparing all the different types of old-growth forests, scientists distilled out four structural components common to all old-growth forests: large live trees, a multilayered canopy, dead standing trees (snags), and downed logs on the forest floor and in streams. Each component describes a physical characteristic of the forest and is not solely dependent on the age, type, or size of the trees. Together the four components define an old-growth forest. If any one of these physical characteristics is absent, the forest is not a true old-growth forest.

Large Live Trees

The first thing you will notice when you walk into an old-growth forest is the huge, massive trees—titanic, some people call them. Rising like granite columns from a rolling green sea of fern and foliage, trees five, six, ten feet across and 250 feet high crease the clouds. Depending on the forest, Douglas-fir, western hemlock, Sitka spruce, western redcedar, and redwood are the dominant trees. Sugar pine, western white pine, ponderosa pine, noble fir, grand fir, Pacific silver fir, incense-cedar, Port-Orford-cedar, and Alaska-cedar play a lesser role. A large individual of any of these trees contains enough wood to build many houses. One redwood reportedly contained 480,000 board feet of wood—enough to build fifty houses. Centuries are needed for a tree to obtain these dimensions. A tree 250 years old is considered young in the old-growth forest; middle age for a giant is 400 to 500 years; old is over seven centuries. For cedars and redwoods, seven centuries is not even middle age—some redwoods reach a millennium and a half, redcedars twice that.

After several centuries of wildfire, windstorms, landslides, floods, and infestation, trees become individualized in their appearance. Lightning has scarred the trunk, wind has snapped off the top, fire has chewed at the base, and rot has hollowed the trunk and limbs. All of this creates the physical variety necessary for a diverse and complex old-growth community of plants and animals. This structural variety is lacking in the

Many plants find growing space
on the broad limbs of a giant tree.
Most of these plants are epiphytic
— that is, they grow on top of the
branch, not actually within the
branch as a parasitic plant would.
These hanging gardens in turn
provide nutrients to the trees and
prime nesting locations for small
birds and mammals.

Ramaria fungus. In November, when the rains return in earnest to the ancient forest, an incredible array of mushrooms pushes past the duff and pops from rotting logs to become visible to the searching eye. These were found in the Coast Range of Oregon.

The banana slug is a Northwest native and a harmless permanent resident of old-growth forests. Although it is an omnivorous plant eater, it is seldom the garden nuisance its brown, introduced slug-cousin is.

Collybia fungi are a widespread genus of mushrooms. This species prefers rotting conifer stumps, as is the case here. MacDonald State Forest, Oregon.

A formerly suppressed western
hemlock growing rapidly in a light
gap created by a fallen giant.
Wind, the typical cause of such
falls, is an agent of plant diversity
in old-growth forests.

Redwood trees represent some of the largest and oldest bundles of life ever to be on earth—some more than 300 feet tall and well over 2,000 years old. Redwood grove, Redwood National Park, California.

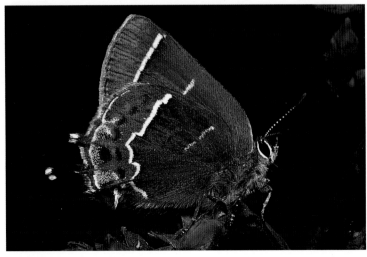

White trillium and swordferns are widespread throughout old-growth forests and can hardly be missed on a spring walk through the ancient trees.

Mistletoe hairstreak, when a caterpillar, is a parasite on dwarf mistletoe but is in turn parasitized by several species of wasps. (Photograph copyright Dave McCorkle.)

managed, cookie-cutter stand of trees. Old-growth forests look mangled and unkempt. They have trees with broken tops where eagles nest, multiple leaders that shelter an owl's nest, dead limbs for osprey to perch on, and a hubbub of holes of many different sizes that shelter both nesting birds and hibernating bears.

Large live trees also produce prodigious quantities of food. Western hemlock produces cones every year and provides a steady source of food for crossbills, siskins, and finches. Douglas-fir produces heavy yields of seeds only every five to seven years, but during those years the seedeaters thrive. Squirrels, moles, voles, and mice also harvest the cones that fall to the forest floor and stash them away for times that are lean.

The large limbs of these forest giants are often a couple of feet in diameter. The constant litterfall of lichens, bark, and dead needles from above eventually accumulates on these limbs to form what scientists call a perched soil. Mosses and ferns germinate to hold the mass together, creating a miniature garden 250 feet above the ground. These perched gardens are havens for wildlife and a boon to the tree itself. The mammals of the canopy use them for loafing, eating, hunting, and sleeping. To birds, in particular the ocean-feeding marbled murrelet, they are convenient nesting sites. The tree benefits from these perched soils by sprouting adventitious roots from its limbs to utilize the rich pocket of nutrients. Limbs big enough to support perched soils are only found on old trees. A planted second-growth forest lacks these canopy gardens.

Multilayered Canopy

The forest is not just a collection of immense trees. For every large tree there are typically three to four more normal-sized trees. These are shade-tolerant trees adapted to grow in the shadow of the larger trees and destined never to reach the latter's dominating size—vine and bigleaf maple, grand fir, Pacific dogwood, Pacific yew—or trees that grow slowly in the shade but prefer more sun and are waiting for an opening in the canopy to obtain their full size—western hemlock and the cedars, for example. This mixture of trees provides the forest with a multilayered canopy—that is, tree boughs throughout the height of the forest. A multilayered canopy is an important structural feature of the old-growth forest. It provides access and cover for animals between the highest trees and the forest floor; it provides ready replacement trees when a giant falls; it ameliorates the forest climate, creating coolness in summer and sanctuary in winter; and it provides a diversity of nest and foraging sites. Northern spotted owls rely on the multiple canopy layers to reduce predation from great horned owls and competition from barred owls. In northern California and occasionally in Oregon and Washington, spotted owls will nest in second-growth forests with remnant large trees as long as the forest has a multilayered canopy structure.

A unique array of plants thrives in the canopy of the ancient forest. Suspended many feet above the ground, inconspicuous dwarf mistletoe grows as a parasite of western hemlock. The mistletoe wedges a rootlike holdfast into the transport cells of the tree, diverting water, minerals, and nutrients intended for its host. If enough mistletoe becomes established in a tree, it can kill a branch or even reduce the growth and vigor of the crown. To find a new host tree, the sticky seeds of the parasite are shot up to fifty feet away by the swollen fruit, which bursts when agitated.

Dwarf mistletoe supports its own microcommunity of animals. Spiders use the stems of the mistletoe to build webs to catch the ants that pollinate the mistletoe's flowers. A tiny rusty brown butterfly, Johnson's hairstreak, feeds on the leaves and stems of the mistletoe. The caterpillar of the parasitic hairstreak is itself parasitized by several kinds of wasps. A similar hairstreak, the dull blue thicket hairstreak, feeds on another species of dwarf mistletoe that parasitizes the Sitka spruce of the coast.

Growing often alongside the dwarf mistletoe is the most common lichen in the ancient forest—lobaria, named for its

Dwarf mistletoe, found in the canopy of the forest, is a parasitic plant, especially on western hemlock. The roots of the mistletoe invade the inner bark of the hemlock branch and extract water, minerals, and nutrients intended for its host. Its seeds can be shot up to 50 feet by the swollen fruit to find a new spot to grow. (Photograph copyright Dave McCorkle.)

The canopy of old-growth forests is characterized by broken treetops, disfigured leaders, and dead wood — all of which ensure the structural complexity necessary for diverse plant and animal communities. Along the Santiam River, Oregon.

Western hemlock growing on a fallen log in Olympic National Park, Washington. Such logs are called "nursery logs" because they provide a good growing environment and nutrients to the young tree.

Dead standing trees, or snags, may remain upright for more than a hundred years after the tree dies. During this time the snag's rotting cavities provide homes for many different animals, including chickadees, flying squirrels, and black bears.

When a tree dies, the nutrients locked within its cells are slowly released by the rotting infiltration of fungi and bacteria. These nutrients are then recycled to other plants and animals.

Bunchberry, a member of the dogwood family, changes to red in October. Some bunchberries overwinter with green leaves to get a jump on food production in spring.

resemblance to lung tissue. Lobaria grows most commonly in the canopy of the ancient forest, where its total weight may reach five hundred pounds per acre. Its dull green prostrate appearance belies its vital function of altering gaseous nitrogen in the air to the nitrate usable by plants. It is one of the few plants of the ancient forest able to make this vital conversion and the primary source of nitrogen for the entire old-growth community. When bits of the lichen break off, they become litterfall on the forest floor; through decomposition, nitrogen is released to enrich the fertility of the soil. Lobaria is found only in forests more than 150 years old.

Snags

When an old tree eventually dies, it may remain standing for 120 years or more, still a vital component in the old-growth forest community. In fact, it has been said that death drives life in the forest. A dead tree creates a light gap in the upper canopy, allowing sunlight to penetrate to the lower canopy and the forest floor. In these light gaps, formerly shaded hemlocks and cedars are released from the dim to compete and gain dominance with the forest giants. A Douglas-fir seedling, not able to grow well in the shade, may now find enough light to push past the surrounding bunchberries and trillium leaves. Vine maple and devil's club grow a bit taller and leafier, and ferns may sprout and carpet the ground. Tree death and the resulting light gaps account for the patchwork arrangement of cover and open space that large animals prefer.

Decomposition and decay eventually enter every cell of the snag and begin to break down and soften the tough wood fiber. Wood-eating bark beetles and metallic wood-borers are often the first invaders of the rotting snag. Drilling perfectly round, bulletlike holes in the trunk, they chomp intricate patterns in the wood, grazing on the inner bark and growing layer for protein and the rotting inner wood for carbohydrates. The holes these beetles make allow other beetles, ants, and burrowing insects access to the nutrients stored in the snag's trunk. One

such insect, unique to the old-growth forests of southwestern Oregon, is the wood-eating cockroach. Scientists consider it a fossil link between cockroaches and termites because in its gut are the same fermenting, wood-digesting bacteria found in termites.

Woodpeckers follow the burrowers and excavate larger holes in search of their insect prey. Chestnut-backed chickadees and Vaux's swifts enlarge the holes for nesting. Flying squirrels occupy the vacant holes to raise their young. Spotted owls, pine martens, fishers, wood ducks, and even bobcats find shelter in larger cavities, and brown creepers and several species of bats build nests under the flaking bark of the old snag. The dead snag, often cursed and commonly cut, is actually an animal apartment house.

Plants also use the snag for home. Fungi of many sizes and shapes sprout from the dying wood as they break down and recycle the stored nutrients. The fungi in turn provide food for more insects and a source of water for animals during times of drought. Red huckleberry and western hemlock commonly germinate on the snag, where they are above the competition on the forest floor and free to use the bank of nutrients in the rotting wood. Fifty tons of snags per acre is typical in an old-growth forest.

Downed Logs

A fortunate Douglas-fir may live to be a thousand years old. As a snag it may stand a hundred years more. When the snag falls, the log will stay on the forest floor another four hundred years. Fifteen hundred years for the cycle of life and death to be complete. Fifteen hundred years for the tree to go and come to ground. Each stage contributes to the forest ecology.

A freshly downed log is certainly an impediment to human travel in the ancient forest. Crossing a series of five-foot-diameter trees becomes a slippery balancing act that creates more frustration than progress. But to a forest mammal these downed logs are a convenient path free of the tangles on the forest floor. Mice, voles, martens, bobcats, mountain lions, and grouse rely on these woody highways. On steep slopes, downed logs slow the erosion of soil, catch a rich accumulation of detritus on their uphill side, and create a sheltered runway on their downhill side.

In summer, when the Douglas-fir ancient forest experiences a prolonged period of drought, the downed log becomes a reservoir of water and food. Salamanders and voles wiggle into the log to find shelter and nutrition. Hemlock seedlings that cannot compete on the forest floor thrive on the rotting log, where they are carried through hard times by the nutrients released by decay and the water stored in the wood. This phenomenon is so common, especially with western hemlock, or Sitka spruce in the north, that such logs that support and nurture the next generation of trees have been given a name — "nursery logs."

The seeds, minerals, nutrients, and water held in the rotting log also represent insurance to the forest. After a severe fire, drought, or the disturbance of logging, the downed log still holds the legacy of the past forest. Research has found that clearcuts that retain downed logs have higher natural seedling regeneration rates than clearcuts devoid of downed logs.

Downed logs are home to countless invertebrates that play a crucial role in the decomposition of plant and animal material and thus in the recycling of nutrients through the forest. The cyanide-producing millipede is common around rotting wood. (Cupping one in your hands and shaking it produces the strong almond odor of cyanide — an effective deterrent to predators.) Millipedes are first in a long line of decomposers that mix plant material and digestive bacteria to break down the plant's tough cellulose structure. One insect's digestive waste, or fras, is another's meal, and thus the detritus passes down the line until the basic elements are released by bacterial and fungal decay and absorbed again by a plant. The omnipresent but overlooked native sow bug continues the decay process and turns out to be the most important animal in the

Red squirrel and Sitka spruce cone, southeastern Alaska.

White trillium, swordfern, and downed logs. Drift Creek Wilderness, Oregon Coast Range.

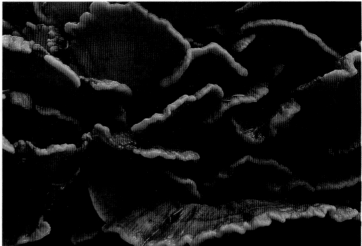

Oregon wood sorrel grows in moist woods from Washington to California. This little wildflower will carpet large areas in the old-growth forest with its shamrocklike leaves and diminutive blossoms.

The scientific name for this little flower is *Moneses*, which translates into "single delight," one of its common names. It grows in wet spots, often in association with rotting wood.

Polyporus fungi are conspicuous members of the decomposition chain that breaks down the dead and recycles it to the living.

Lobaria oregana. As one of the few plants able to convert gaseous nitrogen, which is not usable by plants, into usable nitrate, this modest lichen plays an essential role in sustaining plant growth and soil fertility in the ancient forest ecosystem.

Downed logs serve as a reservoir of water during drought, provide shelter for many insects and small vertebrates, and continually replenish the soil by slowly releasing nutrients.

Vine maple and Douglas-fir reflect
in a still autumn stream in an old-
growth forest in the Washington
Cascades.

Downed logs in streams are vital
to the ancient forest ecosystem.
They provide habitat for many
aquatic animals; they slow the
flow of the water, easing erosion;
they create pools, falls, riffles, and
eddies that fish require; and they
slowly release nutrients to the
stream community. Tongass
National Forest near Juneau,
Alaska.

decomposition chain in converting decaying, mostly rotted logs into the organic parts of soil.

Downed logs in streams create the habitat diversity necessary for a healthy stream community. They create falls, riffles, pools, and backwaters; they capture debris; they lessen the impact of flood waters; and they release their own nutrients into the stream. Woody material is the foundation of the stream community, and native fish and stream invertebrates depend on the physical diversity a downed log creates. Without downed logs, the stream community is impoverished and typically cannot support the native anadromous salmon population so cherished in the Northwest by bears and humans alike.

Logs that are swept downriver add nutrients and physical diversity to both riverbank and aquatic communities. Even in the open ocean, floating old-growth logs continue to be beneficial. A bobbing pocket of life, nourished and protected by the wood, surrounds the floating old-growth log. Fishermen recognize this and find tuna and salmon to be more common around floating oceanic logs.

The physical complexity of the old-growth forest is difficult for many people to appreciate. Scientists have only recently described it and have just begun to understand it. What research suggests is that each structural component appears to be essential to the continued health of the old-growth forest community and that substitutes are not as effective. Nest boxes on live trees cannot replace cavities in an old snag. Chemical fertilizers cannot mimic the complex subtleties of the decomposition process. Artificial dams and rock piles in a stream cannot replace the generations of enrichment from an old sunken log. Only time can effectively replace the snag and enrich the soil and stream. And only time can create an old-growth forest.

In 1952 a forester described the old-growth forest as a "biologic desert." He saw a forest of trees broken and disfigured by age—a forest of rotting logs and weathered snags, a forest smothered in a mossy blanket of decay, where the moldy air was dank and heavy. It was "overmature," "senescent," and "decadent"—a forest long forgotten and gone to waste.

If the intent was to produce a crop of logs, then his was an appropriate description. A plantation of young trees manipulated by foresters for maximum wood production (a "managed" timber stand) produces more wood faster than a five-hundred-year-old Douglas-fir forest. And there is nothing "bad" about this. Managed timber stands are a necessary and vital part of the Northwest landscape. But the managed crop of trees is not a forest in the ecological sense. It is not a heterogeneous mixture of tree species of different sizes and conditions. Its forest floor is not littered with rotting logs. It has few, if any, snags or trees with broken tops, and the ground is not quilted with a verdant cover of wildflowers, fungi, and ferns. Adjectives used to describe the timber stand might be "even," "sparse," "simple," "homogeneous," and "uniform"—just the opposite of "uneven," "broken," "various," "complex," "multiple," and "diverse," words descriptive of the old-growth forest. Nothing is simple or uniform about the life in the ancient forest other than its elegance.

The physical diversity of the old-growth forest translates directly into a higher diversity of animals than is found in the young, managed timber stand. For the first decade or two after a forest is cut and the tree crop replanted, wildlife increases in the area. This is because the first native plants to recolonize the site are typically seed and fruit producers—grasses, berries, and shrubs—that greatly increase the amount of food and protective cover for animals. For the next several decades the young trees grow, their branches intertwining and closing overhead, blocking most of the light from the forest floor. The stand becomes a dark maze of bole and branch without enough light for most herbaceous plants to grow. The stand now lacks shrubby tangle for wildlife to hide in and food for it to consume, and the diversity of animals declines dramatically to less than that of the young clearcut devoid of trees. Here is more likely a "biologic desert." The Northwest's native diverse forest, a haven for many different kinds of plants and animals, is gradually being replaced by managed forests that favor the few and fail the many.

Wildlife needs clutter and chaos. It needs options and opportunities. It needs the slow centuries of growth, nurture, disturbance, and death that produce a complex and unique forest community. Not until the second century of growth does the diversity of plants and animals in a managed stand begin to rise. Two or three more centuries of steadily increasing richness are needed for the forest to reach its maximum diversity. It takes half a millennium, give or take a couple of hundred years, to weave the tapestry—today most acres of managed timber are "harvested" at close to half a hundred years.

Above Winter wrens are diminutive residents of old-growth forests, where they forage among the mossy tangles for bugs and caterpillars. In spring their twittering song dazzles the ear with its strength and complexity. (Photograph copyright Wayne Lynch.)

A young bald eagle feeds on a salmon carcass. Both animals are at times dependent on the pure water of old-growth forests. (Photograph copyright Wayne Lynch.)

Roosevelt elk are a smaller subspecies of elk that lives in the coastal forests within the ancient forest realm. Cutting old-growth forests benefits the elk in the very short term by increasing browse but is detrimental to the animals in the long term by eliminating their winter cover and thermal shelter. (Photograph copyright George Lepp.)

Gray jays live in the lonely corners of the ancient forest. They shy from settlement, but conversely, their bold curiosity toward campers — any handout will do — is renowned. Curiosity, in an environment where food may be sporadic, is a favorable adaptive behavior. (Photograph copyright Wayne Lynch.)

A family of brown bears in coastal Alaska. Bears are "commuter" species in the old-growth community. They are not permanent residents, but they do rely on components of the ecosystem—pure water, for example—and another commuter species, spawning salmon.

The life found in any natural ecosystem can be compared to the life in a city. For the ancient forest this would be a woodland city, but the analogy holds for a prairie, or a desert, or a marsh—each one is a plant city inhabited by animals. Within the old-growth city are a variety of communities in which animals live (the stream community or rotting-log community, for example), work (seed eaters or foliage gleaners, for example), and interact (predators and prey, parasites and hosts, for example).

The longevity and stability of the old-growth city has allowed some animals to be very selective, becoming unique specialists within their community. They may eat only one type of food found only in the ancient forest, as does the red tree vole, or have particular requirements for nesting, such as the northern spotted owl and marbled murrelet. Other animals remain generalists and may live in several cities, commuting to whichever city favors them at the moment. They may find food in several communities but find shelter in the old-growth forest, as elk and deer do; or they may raise a family above treeline but winter in the old-growth forest, as mountain goats do. Some animals, like salmon and bears, are dependent on a particular component of the old-growth ecosystem. Salmon need the clear, gravel-bottomed streams of the old-growth forest to spawn in when they return from the sea. Coastal brown and black bears find shelter and occasionally hibernate inside an old hollow tree and they depend on the salmon to regain weight lost during the long winter.

Of all the animals that live in the ancient forest, a few are restricted to just the old-growth forest, some are most abundant there but are also found elsewhere, and others are more abundant elsewhere but come to the ancient forest at certain times. This does not mean that the forest is more important to some of these animals than others, for there is no luxury in Nature. All the animals that use the ancient forest, no matter how much or how little, do so because it maximizes their chances of survival, and each animal would be disadvantaged if the forest were gone.

Of the specialists inhabiting the old-growth forest, the most well known is the northern spotted owl. Timber interests consider it a gimmick used by "environmentalist whackos" to keep loggers out of the forest. Preservationists revere it as their feathered grail, whose habitat must be protected from any more logging. Why has this unassuming bird come to symbolize the fate of old-growth forests? When the U.S. Forest Service declared the health of the spotted owl population to be indicative of the health of the old-growth forest, the infamy of this bird was assured. Its reputation was further enhanced in June 1990, when the U.S. Fish and Wildlife Service officially declared the owl a threatened species and proposed to set aside over 10 million acres of harvestable timber for its protection. Thus the northern spotted owl has unwittingly become the surrogate for the old-growth forest. Although biologically, the fate of the forest will determine the fate of the owl, politically, the fate of the owl will determine the fate of the forest.

Because of this newfound status, the northern spotted owl is perhaps the most researched and best-understood bird in North America. And yet the most pressing questions about its natural history—what is the minimum amount of forest it needs? what is its minimum viable population level?—can only be answered after the minimum levels have been passed, and then it will be too late.

Despite the questions that still need to be answered, biologists know enough now to make the decisions required to protect the owl. To survive, the best estimates are that each pair of northern spotted owls need at least 1,900 acres of old-growth forest in northern California, 2,200 acres in Oregon, and 3,200 acres in the Olympic Peninsula in Washington. More territory is needed farther north because at higher latitudes the forest produces less food per acre. In northern California, spotted owls have nested successfully in second-growth forests with

The northern spotted owl is a tolerant, almost demure bird that requires 2,000 to 3,000 acres of ancient forest to survive. Predation by great horned owls, displacement by barred owls, and habitat loss from timber operations are its primary threats.

The northern spotted owl was probably never common in old-growth forests but is now largely restricted to them. Legitimate reports of spotted owls found elsewhere are quite uncommon, although a few pairs have nested in second-growth forests that have remnant old-growth components.

remnant large trees and other older-forest attributes, such as a well-developed deciduous understory, but otherwise, nesting is marginal or absent in second-growth stands.

Spotted owls usually do not nest every year, nor are nesting pairs successful every year. In the Northwest spotted owls nest in cavities, snags, or the broken tops of conifers. Reproductive success varies dramatically between years and regions. Reproduction was virtually nil in Washington's Olympic Mountains between 1983 and 1987. In 1988 the Olympic population continued to have a poor nesting season, but 47 percent of the Oregon Cascade population reproduced. In 1989 the Olympic population showed an 80 percent reproduction rate, compared with only 20 percent for Oregon Cascade spotted owls. This fluctuation in nesting success is mostly likely caused by yearly and regional variations in food supply.

The nesting cycle begins with courtship and nest selection in late February and early March. One to three eggs are laid in early spring. Incubation lasts for twenty-eight days and is done solely by the female. The male does all the hunting for the brooding female, usually consuming part of the prey, typically the head, before delivering it to the nest. The male hunts constantly, for his hunting success determines the nesting success of the pair. If the male is an inadequate provider, the female will have to leave the nest to acquire food and the clutch of eggs will die. Researchers report incubating females whistling at their mates to wake them up and stimulate them to hunt.

The owlets leave the nest when they are thirty-five days old and begin to scramble out on nearby limbs; they can fly short distances ten days later. If an owlet drops to the ground at this time, it will climb as high as it can on a downed log and wait there until it can fly to a better perch. Juvenile owls leave the home forest in autumn to join a floating population of unattached adult owls. The mortality rate in juvenile spotted owls is quite high, between 65 and 90 percent. This seems to be due to lack of suitable habitat, which in turn leads to starvation or to predation by great horned owls.

Great horned owls live in the clearcuts and second-growth forests within the ancient forest realm. They are larger and more aggressive than spotted owls and account for a third of juvenile spotted owl mortality. Great horned owls are one of the primary reasons that spotted owls do not and cannot be expected to thrive outside the ancient forest.

A redwood forest in coastal
California shows the physical
diversity characteristic of old-
growth forests. Physical diversity
allows for a variety of ecological
niches and therefore a diverse
animal community.

Wild blueberry is a widespread plant in the ancient forest and a seasonal source of food for many birds.

Food is abundant in the ancient forest to the resourceful animal. Here a black bear has ravaged a Douglas-fir stump infested with carpenter ants.

Tall Oregon-grape, Oregon's state flower. In spring, its lemon yellow flowers are a common sight in old-growth forests; in fall, the grapelike fruit is a source of nourishment for many birds and mammals.

This western red-backed vole and its arboreal cousin, the Oregon red tree vole, are a favorite food of the northern spotted owl. (Photograph copyright Wayne Lynch.)

The cones of western hemlock (the small ones) provide a stable source of food every year, whereas Douglas-fir cones (the large ones) provide a good source of food only every 5 to 7 years.

One of the favorite foods of the spotted owl is the Oregon red tree vole. These stubby mouselike animals are the most specialized rodents in the world and are the high-wire act of the old-growth forest. They forage, mate, nest, grow, and die in the canopy of the cathedral forest, and they do all of this in the dark, for they are nocturnal in habit. Their primary food is the needles of the Douglas-fir. Holding a conifer needle in its front paws the vole will discard the resin ducts and eat the middle of the needle. The ducts are then used to line the vole's twiggy nest.

A basement neighbor of the red tree vole is the western red-backed vole. The red-backed vole accepts a more pedestrian role in the forest than its arboreal cousin although it, too, is a favorite food of the spotted owl. This attractive little rodent spends most of its time on or under the old-growth forest floor. In its subterranean burrow it avoids the vagaries of the seasonal climate, coming to the surface only when conditions ameliorate. Its diet is also peculiarly esoteric. Although it consumes seeds, grasses, and other green plants, the red-backed vole truly relishes truffles.

Truffles are the fruiting bodies of underground fungi, the same kind of fungal fruiting bodies that pigs root for and Europeans savor. Forty-five different types of fungi produce truffles, and thus truffles are common underneath the needles and twigs of the forest floor. Truffles are also beneficial to tree growth. In most tree species, hairlike roots combine with certain underground fungi in a symbiotic relationship called a mycorrhiza. The fungus gets sugars from the tree, and the tree becomes more efficient in taking up minerals and gains protection from pathogens. About two hundred types of fungi form mycorrhizae with trees—evidence of the mutually beneficial nature of the relationship. As it turns out, tree seedlings do not grow as well without their attendant mycorrhizal fungi.

As the red-backed vole scurries through its underground tunnels, it defecates the spores of its just-eaten truffles, thus dispersing the next generation of fungi. The more spores, the

The treetop canopy of the ancient
forest supports a unique
community of plants and animals,
some of which remain virtually
unknown because of their lofty
home.

Pacific treefrog, a ubiquitous and songful frog in moist coniferous forests.

Salmon are animals not usually
associated with old-growth forests,
but they spawn in rivers and
streams enriched and purified by
the ancient forest ecosystem.
(Photograph copyright Wayne
Lynch.)

An immature marbled murrelet in Olympic National Park, Washington. Marbled murrelets are seabirds that nest on the limbs of large trees in the ancient forest. These birds may also be threatened by continued cutting of old-growth forests. (Photograph copyright Gary Mozel.)

greater the possibility for mycorrhizal relationships to form and thus the greater the potential for seedling growth. In the interconnecting relationships between red-backed voles, mycorrhizal fungi, and tree seedlings, we see one strand of the great forest web, or ecosystem. But for there to be many red-backed voles, there must also be rotting logs on the forest floor to provide the voles with cover, a smorgasbord of fungi to eat, and water to drink. The more decaying logs, the more habitat for voles, and by extrapolating a bit further, the healthier the forest and the healthier the spotted owls that nest in the forest and eat the voles.

Dependent on particular components of the old-growth forest for part of their life cycle are the marbled murrelet and the vast Pacific coast salmon population. Commonly seen diving for fish just beyond the ocean breakers, the marbled murrelet is a mottled brown, robin-sized seabird. On the windswept islands of the Bering Sea, the murrelet is a ground nester, but from Afognak Island south, it apparently nests only in old-growth forests. It builds its small nest in dense moss, lichen, or perched soil on a large horizontal limb and commutes to the ocean for food. In Oregon, where the coastal old-growth forest is mostly gone, this commute can be up to an eighty-mile round-trip. Amazingly, only about fifteen tree nests of this bird, each one in old-growth forest, have ever been found. The marbled murrelet, in contrast to its forest neighbor the spotted owl, is perhaps the least-known bird in North America.

The salmon of the Pacific coast are anadromous, hatching in freshwater streams, migrating to the ocean, and returning to the streams several years later to spawn. The baby salmon, or fry, and the returning adults must have clear, cool, gravel-bottomed streams to survive. These characteristics are typical of streams in the old-growth forest, where thick streamside vegetation blocks sediment from entering the water and where fallen trees and their collected debris choke and disrupt the water flow, filtering out suspended solids. Logging the forests

Clear, graveled river bottom in an
old-growth Sitka spruce forest,
southeastern Alaska. Such rivers
and streams are the preferred
spawning grounds of Pacific coast
salmon and the hunting ground of
brown bears and are therefore of
economic importance to the
billion-dollar hunting and fishing
industries of the Northwest.

Three bald eagles on an old-growth stump, southeastern Alaska. Beached, floating, and sunken logs are necessary and contributing parts of healthy river, estuary, and marine ecosystems.

The multilayered canopy of the ancient forest catches the snowfall and provides winter shelter for arboreal mammals and birds. Santiam Pass, Oregon.

The lumpy-backed snail-eater, a predatory beetle of old-growth forests, consumes snails "in house" by sticking its narrowed head into their shells. (Photograph copyright Christian Torgersen.)

around the headwater tributaries, a common practice in the Northwest, negatively affects the salmon by increasing water temperature and sediment load downstream.

Many other animals have as their primary habitat the ancient forest. Very little is known about old-growth forest insects, which some experts estimate number in the thousands of species. The long-legged cricket, with three-inch-long legs, is the only member of its family and is found only in the old-growth forest, but little else about it is known. The funny-bug scorpion fly is a vegetarian (most scorpion flies are predators) and wingless, navigating the forest floor one hop at a time. The trapdoor spider is one of the major predators in the ancient forest, and a fly that is parasitic on the spider is one of the major pollinators of the woodland wildflowers.

One group of insects that has been studied in more detail is the beetles, perhaps because they are relatively easy to find. Lift a piece of old bark, and a beetle is sure to be scurrying away. The black, flightless tiger beetle, *Omus*, is a generalized predator that lives in the decaying plant litter of the forest floor and chomps on whatever critter happens by. A more selective predatory beetle is the lumpy-backed snail-eater. Nocturnal in nature, this inch-long hunter is also flightless and runs over the ground in search of snails. When one is found, the beetle sticks its narrowed head and mouthparts into the snail's shell and consumes it.

The sexton, or burying, beetle is a scavenger. It searches on the wing for mammalian carcasses, following aromas picked up by its ultrasensitive antennae. When a vole, mouse, or shrew is found, the beetle buries it under the forest duff and then lays eggs on the carcass. The larvae hatch to a well-stocked larder and are attended to by the adult beetles. A major problem is that by the time the burying beetles have found the carcass, flies have also. Fly larvae could compete with the beetle larvae and thus reduce the survival of the beetles. To control the unwanted flies, every sexton beetle has tiny symbiotic mites on its back

Pacific giant salamanders, some over 13 inches long, are the largest terrestrial salamanders in the world and are formidable predators of the ancient forest floor. They eat a variety of foods, including snakes, other salamanders, and even small mammals, and are known to growl when angered.

Pine marten, a mostly arboreal member of the weasel family that hunts for squirrels and voles in the ancient forest.

Bobcat hunting the trees for squirrels and voles. The bobcat and its larger cousin, the mountain lion, range widely through many habitats, including old growth, in search of food and shelter.

Black-tailed deer find shelter and winter food in old-growth forests. Olympic National Park, Washington.

The subtle autumn colors of the
forest floor in a northern
California redwood grove. For
such large trees, redwoods have
surprisingly small cones.

A young western hemlock grows from the stump of an old-growth giant. Hemlocks typically sprout on nutrient-rich stumps to lessen competition with the plants of the forest floor.

Young trees rise where old trees
fall. Redcedar and western
hemlock, Bull of the Woods
Wilderness, Oregon.

that eat fly eggs and larvae. When a carcass is found, the mites hop off to consume the fly eggs and larvae as the beetles bury the meat. When the beetle larvae pupate into adults, the mites hop back on for a ride to the next carcass.

Three hundred insect species have been described from the rotting-log community. This community is notable not only for its high diversity, but also for being the only insect community in the ancient forest that has been well studied. Many insects in other microhabitats have not yet been named or studied, and ecologic research is sadly underfunded. In fact, the entire canopy community, including plants and mammals, remains virtually unknown because of its inaccessibility. Insects are the most numerous animals in the forest, but they remain a mystery. How many unique and important cogs in the old-growth community these animals represent remains a major goal for further studies.

More is known about the larger animals that inhabit the old-growth forest. Estimates vary between twenty and one hundred vertebrate species that are closely associated with the ancient forest. Species commonly considered to depend on some part of the old-growth forest during part or all of their lives include fisher; pine marten; Douglas' squirrel; northern flying squirrel; red tree vole; red-backed vole; coast mole; Sitka black-tailed deer; Roosevelt elk; long-eared, hoary, and silver-haired bats; slender, Olympic, Pacific giant, and Del Norte salamanders; tailed frog; northern spotted owl; marbled murrelet; Vaux's swift; brown creeper; pileated woodpecker; western and Hammond's flycatchers; Townsend's and hermit warblers; bald eagle; osprey; northern goshawk; red crossbill; and pine grosbeak. In addition, many more species common in other communities are common in the ancient forest as well. An impressive gathering for a "biologic desert."

A QUESTION OF BALANCE
CHAPTER THREE

To an individual, disturbance is something to be avoided. Regularity and consistency, the roots of predictability, provide few surprises and leave us little to which we need to adapt. Chaos is to be avoided, orderliness sought. Disturbance causes us to be unproductive and insecure, to miss opportunities and lessen our potential.

For the old-growth forest, just the opposite is true. Disturbance is the pump that replenishes the forest's vitality and maintains its physical complexity and biologic diversity. Any disturbance, no matter how small, alters the balance, and the forest readjusts in a dynamic but ever-so-slow musical chair–like movement of life. Light fades or brightens as trees grow and die; damp spots dry and dry spots become wetter; soils creep, roots invade, and nutrient levels vary. Plants and animals survive this perpetual shuffle by seeking locations where they are best able to grow. But as new opportunities are created, old advantages are lost, and the shuffle goes on. A skunk cabbage withers where a vine maple grows. Blueberry invades the brightening shadows. Sunlight pouring through a hole left from a fallen branch defines a red tree vole nest to the scanning eye of an owl, and the glistening dew on a spider's web reveals the hidden net. The blueberry and maple will grow rapidly and prosper in the light; the vole and spider will flee the light and escape to darker corners; and the skunk cabbage will die in the drying ground, its home no longer suitable for its life. Over the years the forest we see as unchanging is in fact dancing to the slow tune of opportunity and adaptation, waltzing with time to the rhythms of change.

Even without a major disturbance, all plant communities gradually change over time. As a plant grows, it creates a slightly different environment from that in which it germinated—more shade, more organic matter, slightly cooler, a bit more moisture. This allows a different plant, better able to take advantage of the new conditions, to grow where the original plant once grew, and thus the plant community gradually changes in a process called succession. As plants change, the animal community changes also. The fox that stalked through the grasses departs to a new meadow as a bobcat pads the overgrown trails.

The start of the successional process usually begins with a disturbance that alters the conditions to which the current communities are adapted. On the grand scale, fire, volcanic eruption, glaciation, and climatic change can obliterate a forest and revert the landscape to just rock and soil. On a smaller scale, earthquakes, landslides, avalanches, treefalls, floods, wind, and insects can selectively change the landscape. No matter the method, the original plant community is altered and a new, better-adapted community replaces it, beginning again the crawl of succession. Be it a branchfall or an ashfall, life will adapt and change and continue. If left alone, the ecosystem will heal itself and begin to revert to the stable climax community.

Because these disturbances occur randomly over time and

Above Calypso orchid in spring—an often unnoticed blossom in the old-growth forest.

The legacy of a fallen log is often apparent from a row of rising trees, for the rotting wood is an ideal nursery for the next generation of trees such as these Douglas-firs and western hemlocks. Middle Santiam Wilderness, Oregon.

The complexity of age, size,
health, and kind within the
ancient forest reflects its diversity
of life and wonder. Crabtree Lake,
Oregon.

The delicate reach of a vine maple
branch with the massive bole of a
western redcedar behind. This
cedar, found along Crabtree
Creek in the Oregon Cascades,
measures 12 feet in diameter.

Salmonberry in bloom after an early May snowstorm. The summertime fruit of the salmonberry is a favorite food of woodland thrushes. H. J. Andrews Research Forest, Oregon.

The infamous rain of the Northwest creates the ideal environment for the giant conifers of the ancient forest.

Rootwad of downed Douglas-fir. Wind, by knocking over trees, creates opportunities for understory plants and is the cause for the variety of tree sizes characteristic of old-growth forests.

place, the primeval forest was a uneven mosaic of different-aged trees with different histories covering different amounts of land. This mosaic gave a rich compositional texture to the forest and provided the diversity of habitats and opportunities necessary for a stable forest ecosystem. Follow any trail in the ancient forest and within a distance of a couple of hundred yards will be areas of giant trees, of small trees, of many snags, of no snags, of downed logs, of thick tangles, and of open forest glades — each area a response to a different disturbance history, but each a part of the forest whole. Whatever the disturbance, at any one time there is ground going to green, meadows growing into forests, and forests dying to ground. The boundless forest of huge trees stretching between the horizons is a myth.

Wind is the primary agent of disturbance in the redwood and spruce/hemlock forest kingdoms because of their proximity to coastal storms, but the effect of the wind is different in each. A strong wind typically knocks over Sitka spruce and western hemlock, tilting their rootwads skyward and exposing the bare mineral soil underneath. Opportunistic plants intolerant of shade and not capable of competing with the thick mossy cover of the forest floor suddenly are able to invade this new growing habitat. Blueberry, vine maple, bigleaf maple, and devil's club flourish around such windthrows.

A strong wind in the redwood forest snaps off treetops but typically does not overturn the roots, for redwoods have shallow intertwining roots that grow into a mutually supporting base. Understory plants surrounding the broken redwood are benefited by the increased light, but new plant invaders are limited by the lack of free soil. The overall effect of wind disturbance is to create a small-scale patchwork distribution of plants, each area responding and adapting to localized, often single-tree changes.

Fire is the primary agent of disturbance in the Douglas-fir kingdom. The west-side forests, contrary to popular opinion, sustain a prolonged summer drought that in severe years can

dry a forest to tinder. An errant lightning strike can then cause a deadly wildfire that races through an old-growth forest with surprising speed, especially if the fire is able to climb through the multilayered canopy and burn the needled crowns. In the west-side forests major burns appear to happen every four to five hundred years — the typical age of the mature old-growth forests in this kingdom. A few groves manage to escape these periodic catastrophic fires and are seven hundred to one thousand years old. In the Douglas-fir region it takes eight hundred to one thousand years for the western hemlock climax community to become established, which is why these communities are so rare. Fire causes a much broader effect on the landscape than wind disturbance and results in a coarser forest mosaic.

More commonly, fires in the west-side forests burn across the forest floor and just scorch the old giants. The thick bark of Douglas-fir and redwood protects them from these "cool" fires, although the trunks often bear the scars of repeated blazes. A ground fire consumes the shrubs and herbaceous plants and burns through the accumulated dead litter on the ground to expose the bare mineral soil in patches. Nourished with ash, this soil makes an ideal growing site for shade-intolerant species such as bunchberry, dogwood, red alder, and Douglas-fir. The predominance of Douglas-fir in the west-side forests is directly caused by the regular occurrence of fire in the region. Without fire to provide an opportunity for Douglas-fir seedlings, western hemlock, a tree that can grow and compete in the shade, would be the dominant tree in the kingdom.

Today the most profound disturbance in the ancient forests is logging. Every day, all day, old trees fall to the logger's saw. Less than 10 percent of the original forest remains. At the current rate, much of the unprotected old-growth forest will be eliminated in ten to fifteen years. Cutting ancient forests and harvesting second-growth timber are ecologically and spiritually different matters. When old-growth forests are logged, part of our natural heritage is lost, and in a simple way we are

This cross-section of an old Douglas-fir log shows the tight growth rings characteristic of old-growth timber. Tight growth rings produce fine-grained wood, which brings a premium price. This type of wood is unique to old-growth trees.

In clear-cutting, after the trees are cut and hauled away, the land is burned to remove brush and is then replanted. Unfortunately, far too many cuts blast through headwater drainages, as is the case here, increasing erosion and siltation downstream, thereby reducing the stream's productivity and the biodiversity of the stream community.

poorer for it. But when a second-growth plantation of trees that has been managed to produce wood products is cut, logging is just the process of removing a crop, much as an Iowa corn farmer would, and is not inherently destructive. In fact, logging is an important and necessary part of life, supplying us with a diverse list of consumer goods, not the least of which are paper and lumber. We will always need wood products and therefore need logging.

Government foresters and private timber industries do an exceptional job of providing the nation with a stable supply of wood. No other country grows wood as well as the United States. Almost 3 billion tree seedlings are planted each year, and no other country legislates and oversees the process more closely. But as in any diverse industry, there are those companies that are sensitive to the land and consider stewardship a part of their legacy and those companies that cut and run and leave nothing behind but eroded slopes and broken promises. Four quarters of financial gain and a huge tax write-off do not seem the proper legacy of a thousand-year-old forest.

But still, as a country, we cannot stop cutting trees. We just have to be more careful with how and what we decide to cut. More intensive management of second-growth timber would lessen the need for wood from old-growth forests. In fact, if once-productive timberland were rehabilitated to again produce timber, jobs as well as wood production would increase. In mature forests, carefully controlled, small-scale logging that leaves more standing trees in smaller harvesting units and that minimizes the use of heavy machinery can and has simulated a natural disturbance regime without strong negative effects on the ecosystem.

But is there a logging technique compatible with the ancient forest, and more importantly, is there enough ancient forest left to support logging? Many people feel that any logging in such a unique and finite environment, no matter how ecologically sensitive, is catastrophic and will eventually consume the old-growth forest: "We've cut enough. Let them cut their

The juxtaposition of severity and
subtlety in the old-growth forest
can at times be overwhelming.
Above Quartzville Creek, Oregon.

Fragmentation of the ancient forest, in which islands of old-growth trees are left surrounded by a sea of clearcuts, diminishes the vitality of the remaining forest and may potentially genetically isolate its residents. Islands smaller than 80 acres cease to function as an old-growth forest community. Douglas-fir seedlings, Snow Peak, Oregon.

plantations — there is plenty of wood out there. Leave the forest alone. Once it is cut it will gone forever." Others feel that is not only possible but desirable: "With what we know now we can selectively cut in the ancient forest, maintain an even supply of logs, and minimize disturbance. Besides, we can always grow more old forests." Have we cut enough? Can we minimize disturbance? Can we grow more? The answer to all these questions is, We just don't know. Either they have not been well studied or they are too subjective to study. Disturbance can be lessened, and it might be possible to replicate some aspects of the ancient forest, but we can't be sure. We will not know when we have cut too much until too much has been cut, and then, unfortunately, it will be too late.

The timber industry also affects life outside the forest. It is the number-one industry in the old-growth region. Revenues from logging fund schools, medical clinics, roads, parks, and municipal services. They support thousands of families, many small towns, and some large counties. All would suffer greatly were the monies from logging to stop. The people involved in the timber industry are not just numbers on a page of statistics. They are families with young children, big bills, and a mortgaged future who genuinely care about the forest and believe that what they are doing is right. Logging is the fabric through which life in these small towns is woven.

In the past, logging to maximize wood production has meant large-scale and repeated disturbances that transform a forest into a crop. Sixty acres of ancient forest can be felled in two weeks by six loggers. It takes another couple of weeks to remove the logs and clear the site and a couple of days to replant it. Add a few applications of chemicals for a couple of years and a thinning after a couple of decades, and in fifty to seventy years the tree crop will be ready to harvest. This method of cutting the forest, called clear-cutting, is the fastest and most economical technique to produce wood, and in a

The demand for wood products powers the march of logging across the landscape. No Northwestern horizon is free from the jagged line of the cutter's mark. The view south, Marys Peak, Oregon.

country and world with an increasing demand for wood products, clear-cutting is the logical choice.

But clear-cutting an ancient forest destroys more than trees. The combination of heavy machinery, dragged logs, and new roads either churns up the soil, compacts it, or displaces it. Downed logs are hauled away, snags are cut, streambeds are exposed, and rootwads overturned. A galloping herd of thousand-pound gophers would be less destructive. Erosion increases, streams are muddied, wildlife is displaced, and people gain access to places humans have never been. Travel by car to the ancient forest and you will not escape the trash and leavings of humans, most of which, by the way, is left not by loggers, but by recreationalists who follow the logging roads. Travel by plane across the ancient forest realm and the patchwork of clearcuts across the forest is conspicuous.

The decision to clear-cut an old-growth forest is based on more than just the inferred quality and amount of wood. An old-growth forest is way past its time of maximum wood production. Although new wood is added each year to an old-growth tree, it is at a much slower rate than a tree only decades old. If you are in the business of producing timber, the more highly productive land you have, the more wood you will be able to produce and the more money you will be able to make. Cutting old-growth forests allows more land to produce more wood.

The demand for old-growth timber and the inadequate supply of second-growth timber sustain the march of clearcuts. But what is so special about old-growth wood products that creates such demand? Only from the ancient forest can clear, fine-grained wood be harvested. Ironically, it is the very uniqueness of the ancient forest environment that produces the wood qualities so valued. After many centuries of sustained growth, the rigors of old age and environmental stress have exacted their toll upon the forest giant. Its lower limbs, long ago shaded and unproductive, have fallen off, and growth has slowed dramatically. Slow growth produces wood with tight growth rings that is clear of knots—"clears" in the lexicon of the lumberman. Clear, fine-grained lumber is the strongest and most valuable wood. Anyone with a guitar or a violin; a deck or a wood-trimmed hot tub; a ladder, railing, or wooden door; molding, shingles and shakes; window trim or outdoor wooden furniture owns an old-growth forest product. And this list does not include the various paper, pulp, particle, and chemical derivatives produced from old-growth timber.

Ninety percent of all clear softwood comes from the Pacific Northwest, and its price has increased 80 percent in the last two years. Because the demand is so great for this high-quality wood and the supply is becoming tighter, a raw log is worth more than the finished product. This is equivalent to saying that a lump of steel is worth more than a car. But buyers from the Asian rim and Europe pay premium prices for the lumber unique to the ancient forest.

This outlook assumes that the only value to a tree is in the wood that it produces. But there are other, harder-to-quantify values. The biological legacy held in the genetic history of each tree ensures the continued viability of today's forests—both natural and planted. The richness of species in the ancient forest acts as a reservoir to replenish adjacent land. The wildlife that the forest harbors has value in its own right. On a more utilitarian level, the health and extent of the ancient forest ecosystem is directly responsible for the health of the region's billion-dollar salmon fishery and the purity of the region's drinking water. Unfortunately, the ecological, recreational, spiritual, and emotional values of the ancient forest are typically discounted or ignored. But how do you assign a value to the reassurance that old-growth forests exist or to the stirrings of awe these forests elicit? And how do you balance these values with a vacant mill or a foreclosed home? These are questions that perhaps only the children of our children's children will have the wisdom to answer.

A managed timber stand of
second-growth trees in the Coast
Range of Oregon. Grown as a
crop of wood to satisfy our
demand for wood products, these
trees were cut in 1990.

This dense stand of second-growth western hemlock on the Olympic Peninsula supports far less animal life than the ancient forest and even less than a new clearcut.

Autumn reflections of vine maple
in the Crabtree Lake Natural
Area, central Oregon Cascades.

Oxalis and redcedar trunk—
both products of undisturbed
centuries.

Vanilla leaf, or sweet-after-death, is widely found in the ancient forests of Washington and Oregon. The name refers to the sweet vanilla aroma of the leaves.

Glacier lilies growing in a rocky clearing serve as a food source for many animals. Black and brown bears dig for their nutritious roots, and deer eat the seed pods.

The subtleties of form and function require time and opportunity. Devil's club in early spring.

Rhododendrons are typical in
undisturbed forests within the
ancient forest realm. Forty- to
sixty-year logging rotations
prevent rhododendrons from
becoming established in second-
growth forests.

The vegetation of a riparian area shelters, nourishes, and ensures a healthy aquatic community. Buffer zones protecting old-growth forest streams from logging operations are becoming increasingly common.

The sinuous limbs of the vine maple often grow into a dense tangle, a habit from which the tree earned its name.

Natural regeneration of western hemlock and Douglas-fir after old-growth Douglas-fir and redcedar have been logged can be prolific. The forest's structural diversity — snags, shrubs, and downed logs — apparent in the untidiness of the regenerating forest, is as ecologically important in a young forest as it is in the ancient forest.

Young and old western hemlocks
mark the continuation of a forest
that may be 10,000 years old.
What will be its next 10 millennia?

Ecologically, of course, the replanted forest is not the same as the ancient forest, and the unique animal life harbored in the ancient forest must move to another grove of old trees, try to adapt suddenly to a new environment, or die. But as the demand for wood products has increased and the scars of clearcuts have multiplied, the remaining patches of old-growth forest are becoming smaller and more widely dispersed. This fragmentation of the forest dislocates the interconnected web of forest communities, isolating groves of ancient forest within a sea of clearcuts and young trees. The northern spotted owl has been particularly impacted by this fragmentation. In addition to the declining amount of its habitat, other primary threats to the northern spotted owl are territory displacement by the larger and more aggressive barred owl and predation on the spotted owl's young by great horned owls. Both barred and great horned owls are not as specialized in their habitat preferences as the spotted owl and therefore thrive in altered forests. Their populations have increased as ancient forests have been cut and replaced by younger forests, further threatening the survival of the remaining spotted owls. One-third of juvenile spotted owl mortality is caused by great horned owls.

Even just a road passing through an old-growth forest can impact the forest ecosystem. Red tree voles commonly traverse the forest on touching boughs, and a road limits such travels. If the remaining forest fragment is less than eighty acres or so, it ceases to have many of the functions of an old-growth community of larger expanse. If the remnant old growth is too distant from other old-growth forests, animal populations lose contact, weakening their genetic resource and threatening the success of juvenile dispersal. The remaining old-growth forests in the Olympic Peninsula of Washington are now biologically isolated from the ancient forests of the Cascades. No replenishment of species to maintain the genetic vitality of plant and animal populations is possible now, and species richness and diversity in these ancient forests will surely diminish.

One thousand years for a tree to grow and come to ground in the emerald forest. Twenty-five minutes to cut it down. Less than 10 percent of the ancient forest remains, 2 percent of the redwoods. Are there not values of the ancient forest beyond those that can be penciled on a ledger sheet? Is there enough now set aside to preserve the rich ecological diversity of these ecosystems? Should the remainder to be cut for the sake of community economic stability? Or will the eyes and hearts of the future mourn the last great forest?

These questions cannot be answered, but yet they must be. The ancient forests belong to all of us — they are our heritage, and we all have a say on their future. The retired folks in Pilot Knob, New York, or Whitehall, Pennsylvania; the students in St. Paul, Minnesota, or Sweet Home, Oregon; and the toddlers in Knoxville, Tennessee, all have an equal voice in the fate of the ancient forest. But one must care in order to speak and speak in order to be heard. If you do nothing, then politicians, those least qualified to decide, will. Let your voice be heard, for silence has sharper teeth than the sawyer's blade.

Further Reading

Ambler, Julie, and John Patt. *Guide to the Middle Santiam and Old Cascades.* Corvallis, Oreg.: Marys Peak Group, Sierra Club, 1981.

Becking, Rudolf W. *Pocket Flora of the Redwood Forest.* Covelo, Calif.: Island Press, 1982.

Canadian Western Wilderness Committee. *Carmanah: Artistic Visions of an Ancient Rainforest.* Canada: Summer Wild Productions, 1990.

Cissel, Diane & John, and Peter Eberhardt. *50 Old-growth Day Hikes in the Willamette National Forest* (map), 1991.

Dittmar family. *Visitors' Guide to Ancient Forests of Western Washington.* Washington, D.C.: Wilderness Society, 1989.

Ervin, Keith. *Fragile Majesty: The Battle for North America's Last Great Forest.* Seattle: The Mountaineers, 1989.

Henrie, Charis. *Old Growth Forests: A Casual Hikers' Guide.* Portland, Oreg.: World Forestry Center, 1990.

Houle, Marcy Cottrell. *One City's Wilderness: Portland's Forest Park.* Portland: Oregon Historical Society, 1988.

Kelly, David, and Gary Braasch. *Secrets of the Old Growth Forest.* Salt Lake City: Peregrin Smith, 1988.

Lilja, Irene, and Dick Lilja. *Siuslaw Forest Hikes.* Albuquerque: Heritage, 1990.

Maser, Chris. *Forest Primeval: The Natural History of an Ancient Forest.* San Francisco: Sierra Club Books, 1989.

Maser, Chris, and James M. Trappe. *The Seen and Unseen World of the Fallen Tree.* Washington, D.C.: U.S. Department of Agriculture, 1984.

Norse, Elliott A. *Ancient Forests of the Pacific Northwest.* Covelo, Calif.: Island Press, 1990.

Pyle, Robert Michael. *Wintergreen: Listening to the Land's Heart.* Boston: Houghton Mifflin, 1986.

Sullivan, William L. *Exploring Oregon's Wild Areas.* Seattle: The Mountaineers, 1988.

Sullivan, William L. *100 Hikes in the Central Oregon Cascades.* Eugene, Oreg.: Navillus Press, 1991.

Wood, Robert L. *Olympic Mountains Trail Guide.* Seattle: The Mountaineers, 1984.

Wood, Wendell. *A Walking Guide to Oregon's Ancient Forests.* Portland: Oregon Natural Resources Council, 1991.